Unearthing the Road to Rome

By: Timothy Hollins

Table of Content

1. Acknowledgements   pg. 3

2. Mission   pg. 4

3. Pink Elephant with Two Trunks   pg. 5-7

4. De facto (blog)   pg. 8

5. Appropriate Adaptation (blog)   pg. 9-10

6. Ideology (Beliefs) Opposed to Facts   pg. 11-13

7. Mockingbird's Canticle (poem)   pg. 14

8. Sunday's Sun (blog)   pg. 15-16

9. The Eight-sided race   pg. 17-18

10. Can I live? (blog)   pg. 19

11. The Non-tangible (in theory)   pg. 20-21

12. Expired: Reality or Dream? (blog)   pg. 22

13. Natural Order   pg. 23-24

14. Dress-Code (blog)   pg. 25-26

Acknowledgements: First and foremost I'd like to give praise to Divine's protective hedge over my lost soul and His grace and guidance in all areas of my life. I'd like to thank family and friends, and of course Anthony 'Doc' Staples for the many shared ideas and thought provoking hours of conversations we engage in. Respect and my deepest love to my inner circle (small but it's there lol)!

Mission: Succeeding in a mental resurrection to recondition the masses of twisted and decaying minds by exposing society collective to centuries of unhealthy, racist ideologies (whether knowing or unknowing; implicit or explicit) and daily practices, and reversing this pattern of corrupt, wicked, and terminal mental illness which has produced a zombie existence and numbness towards racial diversity in the world's population. I toil to expose the illogical, unjust, and inhuman treatment of the Black race being manifested though the oppressor's dictation that is orchestrated in every facet of society's conscious and subconscious whereas the transference of these guilts, lies, even intuition of the oppressor, are bestowed upon the oppressed. After demolishing and crumbling such power structures can the Black race work to build and replace all of the before mentioned with injections of truths, rooted spirituality, love for all, and a mental protein diet of daily practices in self-reflection and self-respect.

Timothy LSohl Hollins
Author/Poet

When the unified field annihilates the killing fields
-albeit Divine's will
And counterculture ideas cleanse the old minds
Ambivalence within is no more...but peace
That's the moment civilization, as we know it, has come to an end
LSohl

Pink Elephant with Two Trunks

There are countless issues, problems, and foci when addressing the various races that make up today's society. These subjects are readily and overtly addressed through studies of Cultural diversity, anthropology, psychology, and a number of other social sciences. Yet many will deviate from the race discussions, not so much with identifying these differences among the races and cultures or the races' origins, but more so when addressing the psyche of individuals that project a dislike towards these differences, and project feelings of superiority in regards to innate rights bestowed upon all living people...the human rights of liberty, justice, and equality. This is where the uneasiness lies in a multitude of mankind, making it hard to internalize and overtly admit to this obvious issue. The ones traveling this road with feelings of entitlement and superiority over other races readily embrace racism...a road often traveled but considered taboo to open discussions.

Society lives in a transparent state of denial when it comes to racism. It appears that many would like to believe this darkness no longer exist, and in discussing the true undertone of this society, it will bring about universal misfortune that will declare all that address the subject as a racist! Maybe the masses would prefer to live the fallacy of a 17th century colonial lifestyle believing in witches and apparitions...claiming these supernatural entities and satanic servants were the cause of all social discord. Or maybe present society believes in Pandora's box of mischief, disease and misfortune. Paraphrasing Malcolm X, one of the greatest Black leaders in American history, he stated that *the only way to resolve this growing race problem in America is for the White man and Black man to meet at a table then openly and honestly discuss their issues with one another without holding back in fear of hurting the other's feelings.* This would be the beginning of true reconciliation and healing between the two races. But those that tackle this pink elephant with two trunks in society's parlor are considered trouble-making radicals; influential discords to contemporary social harmony.

Prior to the antebellum epoch, one will notice this topic was overtly discussed when pertaining to the so-called White race and slave relation due to the latter being classified as property, primates, objects of possession, and additions to the slave-masters articles of livestock. So in relegating the Black slaves to sub-human, discussing racial views and maintaining the status in quo were addressed under comforting atmospheres to the white collective.

AMERICA, you know not the magnitude of your sins, nor shall they ever be notated or engraved in your history...these perpetual crimes against humanity! It has forever been clear that consciousness, moral psyche and spirituality elude you. You are, at whole, components creating a 'dark'; the fallen sides of Divine's grace. What reprisal, what wrath awaits thee as you lurk in your wayward, destructive and deadly transition on, in, and over the earth? Your sight sees clear nothing, not even partials of particles when referencing justice and true liberty for all! Truth is outweighed tenfold by the lightest feather as lies, and deceit rest comfortably on your fork tongues. What serpent beithe you to slither deadlier than the mamba then thirst for more poison yet call your actions civilized? Each word you write, recite, think, and create makes the citizens of an educated society gasp from your polluted venom. Your promises are motives, pretexts to your grand, evil schemes. I record my opinions as truths that you are but the blood and doubts that straddle, trample, and stunt love, liberty, truth, and dreams. And I am, as you that read this text, a byproduct of YOU! Now I stand to self-reflect in an effort to correct the decaying mentally and conditioning forced upon me. I come to expose America, the mythomane, and propagate you into a state of fruitfulness, a mensch to all society. I am the prototype for newness, boundless flight, fresh air, freewill, and ascension.

Today's White society attempts to disguise their racist Jim Crow views and practices through racially coded language and laws. The educated racist need not belch out derogatory labels like "nigger", "coon", and "darkie" when referring to the Black population. White politicians and lawmakers on local, state, and federal levels replace such labels with media-friendly terms like "thugs", "criminals," and "hoodlums". They have popularized terms and phrases and associated them with the Black community... phrases like "law and order", and "get tough" laws when dealing with "criminals" (largely people of color).

"Law and order" became the adopted phase of the elite and government officials to legally continue racial inequalities and injustices upon Blacks when they saw a political and legislative change occurring for Blacks and people of color during the Jim Crow era...a change that would promote a sense of justice for the Black race that had been shackled by American society.

Today's lower caste system created for Blacks is defined not so much by racial hostility but more so by racial indifference (lack of compassion and caring). This is what makes the issue of racism so hard to digest by many Whites today. Western society cannot fathom the reality of their "white privileges". They argue that the social and justice playing fields are equal and leveled between the races. They blindly present arguments of "hardships" and "prejudices" they encounter daily (weight issues, bullying, lack of financial resources, etc.) and compare such to those of being Black in a White American racist society. They would believe their inconveniences are equal, if not worse, than the injustices that plague the Black race.

This same displacement and disconnect the White world both consciously and subconsciously carry around is what causes them to impose their "will", "ways", and "opinions" on every people of color. In 1803 Britain settled southern Australia where the Tasmania people who had occupied the area for 10,000 years lived peacefully. The Tasmanian tribe was 5000 members strong. Britain eventually killed off the entire tribe through murders and diseases they brought along with them in their effort to "colonize" an indigenous people that lived healthy lives before the White invasion. I must point out that along with the British civilized teachings, they also raped the Tasmanian women. This had to be viewed as such a high moral tactic by both Britain and these beautiful people of color.

The uneducated and those that lack proper understanding of historical facts, discernment, and empathy for the atrocities waged against the Black race will often produce the same watered-down argument claiming the genocides employed on other races by barbarians such as Mussolini, Stalin, Hitler, Pol Pot, Lenin, Nero, Caesar, Genghis Khan, and the Roman emperor Caligula are equal to or more horrific than what people of African decent faced/face in America. Though these monstrous men were responsible for such horrific and hideous acts of social and political repression, depopulation through executions, forced sterilization, famine, etc., and the torturing of millions during their 'short' reign/dictatorship in history, still none can be compared to that of the American Black slave. Captive Africans forced on western shores reluctantly awaited a black-hearted, soulless creature labeled 'master' in a deep-rooted hate and abyss known as America.

The Africans kidnapped and transported to America were enslaved physically, and mentally broken for generations on in. African families, generation after generation for hundreds of years, were born into slavery in America, and under the most inhuman conditions in terms of physical, spiritual, social, and mental abuse. And under these conditions forced upon the enslaved Blacks for numerous generations, a mental conditioning and recoding were established in both races; Whites conditioned to feel superior to Blacks and all races in society through their irrational developed ideologies and daily practices which instituted an ungodly movement defined in the many aspects of racism, while Blacks where conditioned to feel subhuman, inferior, and helpless even after being manumitted from chattel slavery.

As the generations of Blacks born into American slavery unfolded, enslaved Africans were transformed into American Black slaves or slaves of African decent. Even a partial fairness and fraction of discernment to this truth can only bring a beacon of understanding to what Blacks faced on these western shores, and what Blacks collective still face today. The treatment of Blacks in American cannot be likened to that of any other people that was brutalized and murdered. A mass murdering and physical annihilation of a people whether just or unjust is totally unacceptable in any moral and god-fearing society, but to annihilate a race collective way of thinking, spirit, intuitions, language, religion, and logic through generations of forced conditioning during slavery which in turns redefines that collective race's (Blacks) every interaction is far more tragic.

De facto (blog)

Given the gained interest in police killings and brutality of countless Blacks and people of color, many Whites feel unmoved or alarmed by such inhuman injustices until these acts of barbarianism lie at the unwelcome mats of their front doors. But should this sway in interest and opinion come as such a shock to anyone who has vested the smallest attention to America's history? During the colonies Declaration of Independence from Britain, the colonists visceral feelings towards Britain's act of tyranny and denial of liberty bestowed upon them where somehow disregarded when it came to the African slaves they held as personal property. This hypocrisy was pointed out by the African slaves as well as some of the Whites own colleagues, including Samuel Johnson as he stated, "...how is it that we hear the loudest yelps for liberty from the drivers of Negroes?" This nation was built on racism and hypocrisy, so should the contradictory views of White society come as a shock when referencing Black issues which are certainly not seen as society issues? Blacks have to wake up emotionally, mentally, and spiritually and recognize we are an unwanted enclave within these United States. So much has changed since those days of the founding fathers (laws and practices) but just as much have remained unmoved. De facto versus de jure could never be more evident when addressing race policies, laws, issues, and practices in the United States.

Love Divine and self first in order to truly love others!

Appropriate Adaptation (blog)

How should I start this I wondered?   How can I open minds to relate and convey what I've been struggling with for so many years...my people? Every issue encountered in this life whether good or bad revolve around the issue of race. While most, in relations to the latter, are ascribed to the Black race by the so-called majority Whites in Western society. And we as a collective, blindly clutter and stumble along daily as if we have no earthly clue of the negative stigmas and dehumanizing images that have been branded upon us as a whole by the before mentioned...no matter what social stratosphere we reach. Why do we ignore the bright neon signs of hatred, distrust, and injustices practiced daily by White America and others, towards the Black race? Why do so many of my Black brothers and sisters contribute to these images that only devalue and deface us as a collective? Often times, when people are placed in a particular category or have a stigma placed on them by the "civilized society" they **exist in**, psychologically those individuals tend to embrace the stigma; case-in- point as seen by black teens being stigmatized as thugs and criminals, so many of them embrace the life as a way to rebel the society they learn to resent and label a pariah or living hell.

Well, I assume if we start with self first and work on fixing and healing all that is broken and sick within us mentally, emotionally, and spiritually, then and only then can we begin our journey towards proclaiming we are a strong and prideful Black race.

Much of my frustration is around how we, as a race, feel the need to be accepted. How we, as a race, have allowed ourselves to be made to feel uneasy, unpatriotic, and ashamed to White America's discomfort in remembering this country's true bloody and savage history, barbaric legacy, and ungodly ways of life even at present. We are said to be "*holding on to the past...that didn't happen to you...you aren't a slave...I wasn't a master.*" And we have bought into these asinine questions and statements I refer to as call-and-answer discourse.

How can we embrace every culture but the one that was almost erased from us...our very own? How can we add to the disconnect of our children by not educating them properly in the true history of America and in our history, and then readily procreate but are not willing to protect by any means necessary the lives we bring into this cruel and unjust society that breathe racial tension in every aspect of living as we know it? How can this be? How can we take to social media, televised news networks, radio airwaves and such and speak in favor of the brutalities, killings, and atrocities that have been plaguing our people by the hoofs of a white supremacy network collective? Why do we try to find justification for their demonic actions against us...then we lay blame at the feet of the sheep/victims; our own brothers, sisters, mothers, fathers, and babies?

We do this because we have been conditioned well! Watching the news and reading the papers, White America makes no effort to hide the disparities in justice and treatment between them and the Black race on a moral, social, political, economical, educational, and employment level in this "civilized" arena. (I say civilized in satire). The war on drugs, which was racially coded with a pretext for mass incarceration of Blacks and people of color, a pretext to destroy Black men, women, children, and families, and a pretext to criminalize poverty-stricken Blacks has been re-evaluated. Now, with the growing numbers of suburban white kids using and dying from drugs like heroin, civilized society has decided to look upon what was once considered a criminal drug epidemic plaguing the Black ghettos and neighborhoods, and redefined it as drug problem, an issue of concern...a sickness that needs treatment. Again, they make no quarrels in hiding this. Not surprising at all to the minds of conscious Blacks and radical Whites.

I read of a case somewhere in these United States where a White college student was arrested for public drunkenness, public disturbance, lewd behavior, resisting arrest, etc., and the arresting officer used excessive force and choked the young fellow. The officer was immediately fired! The consensus among White America regarding this incident was the officer was totally out of line and a *loose cannon*. Fast forward to more current accounts of excessive and unnecessary force and tactic when the young Black girl was tossed, dragged, and thrown across a classroom, but the same civilized society questions the child's upbringing. Why wasn't the upbringing of the college student in question? But what disturbs me more over is some members the Black race taking a fiddle playing, boot-tapping, and shoe-licking stance along side their White counterparts attempting to point out what this little GIRL could have possibly done before hand to provoke such an attack...precipitating factors.

I can tell you what she did that may have caused the coward to respond the way he did...absolutely nothing. Nothing can justify an adult, male or female, (rational and logical) acting primal towards a child (mostly irrational and illogical in thought process and maturity by NATURE when referencing defiance). So why again do we do this as Black people...because we don't want to offend our White inhibitors. We sung, begged, graveled, and many fought for equality, but today's generations dare actually demand these God given rights to all. You see, the timid, cowardly, and mundane Blacks feel we cannot let the White race think we navigate the same stratosphere as them. No! Never do that! We must always know "our place" whether we do this conscious or subconsciously.

We are a consciously sick race, my friends! We are but walking cadavers, denizens to a fleshy mobile unit with no trace of intellect...feeble-minded flesh consumers- a pariah to society collective.

But wait! No! No! I cannot wear the bloody leather to those uncomfortably tight shoes. Those shoes never fit my sole/soul. I am that sui generis mensch, a lone wolf observing a pack of mutts still pulling the master's sled. I've recognized what the politics of respectability were/are, and I firmly rejected and ignored such. I adapt only to what I feel is right. Unlock your mental chains and be free!

Dichotomy of the River Banks
...Oh, the scent of the river that flows
The scent of a society gags, smothers, strangles as it imposes and enslaves
Old minds wage a war with young revolutionaries
A kindred to rebel spirits so I dance young
The dichotomy...
LSohl

Ideology (Beliefs) Opposed to Facts

To recondition a mind, one has to, first, travel back in time to visit the prehistoric past in order to understand how we have arrived at our present status. Secondly, we must become clear observers of our present in an effort to achieve a brighter future. We accomplish each of these tasks by starting with the fundamental methods in educating a society. We all began our journey to learning as infants and adolescents through our innate sensory experiences of touching, seeing, feeling, smelling, and hearing. We collect mental data using these senses along with our instinctive need to explore, and digest these empirical experiments into recognition learning and conditioning. As we approached society's recognized age for elementary schooling, we gain systematic programming from the organized learning institutions. We learned basics concepts in these institutions, concepts that separated scientific facts from beliefs and opinions.

Science is the study of facts that govern the operation of general laws. Within science, lies theories and hypothesis, which are defined as educated guess (beliefs). These notions remain beliefs until proven as factual through a series of tests and experiments that will conclude the same results. Science, in general, deals with numbers, experiments, and equations to prove and produce a consistent outcome when applied each and every time, making these experiments factual.

Beliefs, on the other hand, are not facts. Beliefs are opinions of each individual, or shared opinions by a group of people. Example: On a rainy day, one cannot state is it factual that the day is horrible due to the *fact* that someone else perceives the rain as a joyous occasion. The description used is of a subjective nature. So, this statement is an individual opinion produced by independent feelings the person experiences during said occasions. Again, beliefs are merely opinions and have been commonly used to give birth to countless practices in society. For instant, when a group of individuals share similar or the same beliefs in supernatural existences, a religion is birthed.

In religion, practices and ceremonies are established to pay reverence to this supernatural existence. So let us explore the evolution of religion in an attempt to awaken the masses to the ***fact*** that religion as you know did not start with Christianity, Islam, Buddhism, or even Hinduism (which is considered the oldest religion although Hindus do not claim this to be a religion).

The anatomically modern humans/anatomically modern Homo sapiens have performed ceremonies dating as far back as 34th century BCE (before the common era of Christ). These Homo sapiens (bipedal primates that are characterized by their capacity to learn by strategizing, manipulating and enhancing their environment, and developing languages and tools...wise men) performed rituals of burying their dead as a sign of empathy after the epoch of excarnation. *Note: when referencing the taxonomic family of hominins, all prior related species have become extinct. I emphasize this point to make it clear life did not start with the Homo sapiens.*

Religion, as we know it, has been recorded by methods of formal writings in history for a mere 5000 years or so. But practices, as stated above, have long been in existence through primitive oral communication and art long before the evolved humans we are at present. So we can conclude that religion, as with humans and every other facet of life, has evolved. Then why has society put great emphasis on propagating different present-day religions as origins to our existence? How does this false campaign by the European race affect the multitude of cultures and the conditioning of minds collective? Let's examine Christianity. History records the Roman emperor Nero's persecution of Christians due to the Great Fire of Rome. Nero blamed Christians and their strange worshipping for the fire. Rulers and townspeople persecuted Christians at will for centuries alike for various reasons until the passage of the Edict of Milan, which denounced persecuting the followers of Christian faith. During these times and the times that followed, Christians (whose religion was formed around many Zoroastrian beliefs) devised a campaign that brought about changes in their beliefs in an effort to make Christianity acceptable by a resisting society they resided within. Why change what is true? Changes seemed necessary for the survival of this dogma. So this religion, like most, evolved throughout time to exist and co-exist within the established society. The same way Romans viewed Christianity and made it an acceptable way of life to persecute Christians, but later relieved themselves of such harsh, unfair, and inhumane ways of thinking, present day Christian society need to follow this example in regards to racism and other religious practices.

Today, Christianity has the largest following worldwide. But what if the Romans stuck to their original beliefs when pertaining to people of the Christian faith? Would this religion be extinct? Why did they, the Romans, feel the need to force their ways and religion on a people that obviously viewed things different? The problem isn't with a belief or view on religion. The problem comes when one forces their views and beliefs onto another with different beliefs and customs. What makes the majority or the minority way the right way when it comes to a belief? I whole-heartedly believe in God. This is my belief, which rest comfortably in my mind, heart, and soul as a fact! I, along with the masses, have programmed into my all, that my belief is indeed a fact. I'm conscious of this belief/fact of mine, and this is what separates me from so many others to a point I don't involve myself in religious debates which are often times emotionally charged arguments...not debates. I try to stray away from religions. I believe that whatever makes any individual better in the aspect of spirituality, it shouldn't matter how that person gains this connection. Does it truly matters which road was taken to get to Divine as long as all roads lead to Him? That is the ultimate goal. Preachers, Ministers, Bishops, Reverends, etc., all emphasis at one point or the other how they, your parents, love-ones, friends, cannot get you into this Heaven! They explain that only you have control of your eternal resting place. With this being said, it all comes back to self again! You are in control of your spiritual connection with God. Again, the problem exists with the forcing of one's beliefs onto others of different beliefs, rituals, and customs. So why would the White race forcefully place this religion above all others and into the lives of different races? Their actions are racist, both conscious and subconscious! Given the dogma, Christianity, they present, Whites explain Jesus as the Messiah/Son of God. They have lied and depicted Him to be a White man with blue eyes and long flowing blond hair. This is the age-old debate, but it does hold relevance to what I'm suggesting. Using the text, the Bible, that they use we have learned all throughout it's holiness that the people in the region mentioned in Biblical times were people of color, and Jesus was a man of color. One with a morsel of any intellect would have to ask why then would he be depicted worldwide as a White Jesus? The answer is obviously superiority! This depiction of the Holy Messiah is to support their pseudo-ideology that they are the superior race. This sense of superiority trails deep into our (global) history.

The society we live in, and everything existing in, on, and around it, evolves constantly. This has been the case since the existence of this small planet. Evolving is a method of adapting to the surroundings of the time. This does not make one species or race superior to the next. Each plays a vital role in the life of all. The father of evolution, Francis Galton, only strengthened the false beliefs of Europeans being the superior race to all with his theories on evolution concluding that everything came into existence and evolved by conflict...only the strong survives. Whites killed off indigenous people whenever they invaded and intruded upon already settled grounds...grounds they viewed as discovering and colonizing. They survived.

Mockingbird's Canticle

Can you hear the mockingbird's cry in this fierce, raging storm
Or its feet relentless patter in the puddles afterwards in yellow sun
Was it dance or trauma or a desperate search for calm
Sing on and mimic my song, mockingbird

What words lie beneath the soils I walk
What untold stories? What despair? What glory to squawk?
Why fly so near the blood leaves on blood trees
where strange fruit bears resemblance to me, mockingbird?
Sing on and mimic my song you silly bird

Magnolia rust then polished for the turn of a new century
What lust and inhuman atrocities spirit the growth; the roots
Strange fruit indeed wiped clean from guilty memories
Spring winds carry the must and terror that stained the under-sleeves
Yet that mockingbird continues to mimic me
-sing on

LSohl
11/17/14

Sunday's Sun (blog)

Sunday morning wake-up and I'm awaken to the world. A bright blinding sunshine exposes the world in both a subjective and objective way...truth versus lie, fact versus opinion, rational versus irrational ways of thinking and interacting. This is what I wake to. Maybe this is the reason my views and OPINIONS are sought out by the ones that know me. People often ask me of my take on different social and political topics, and no matter what the discussion I redirect them back to self.

We find ourselves in disagreement with so much of society and how it is ran; from our families, jobs, religions, politics, police, etc...we are at ends in one way or the other. The current situation with police brutality and/or fatalities in this country is a hot topic especially among Blacks. I'm going to use the term "current" very loosely due to the fact this (police killings being racially motivated or an abuse of authority and power) has always been the case towards minorities, especially Blacks in America. So when I see all the posts of these injustices tagged with old Tupac or Marvin Gaye lyrics as if these artists prophesied such occurrences, it only saddens me to the reality of how blind so many of us have been for so long. These wrongful acts and atrocities, like so many others, have long existed.

Social media and videophones only expose such things on a broader stage...the show is the same. But I won't tackle this right now because what I see are individuals- individuals (each of us) that take to these social sites and put importance on things like shoes, phones, cars, (hell, it has gotten so bad that we even want fb to see our dashboard light displays) houses, all kinds of material things but rarely are we posting about good morals we practice and past down to our children. We find it entertaining and magnetic to be clowns in front of the camera, for our women to be half-naked, for our men and children to assault each other, for us to degrade our beautiful sisters, but then we will post short quotes we have skimmed across that suggest we came from a race of kings and queens.

I don't feel there is anything wrong with being proud of things you have worked hard for, but let's keep them in perspective. You see, maybe when we buy our sons that pair of Jordan sneakers and explain to them that they are nice clothing accessories and nothing more, but they won't out last or shine longer than respect, dignity, and pride in self then that pair of Jordan's won't be seen as an item to fight and even kill for. Maybe if we teach our daughters the beauty of their brains, the complexity of their bodies as a Divine art then they won't feel the need to expose so much of their physical. And just maybe if our broken men knew what real strength they held in spirit and heart, we wouldn't try to glamorize images of players and pimps which only causes more distrust and conflict in ourselves and our women.

So here we are again meeting with the very nature of humans...conflict. No matter what policy, procedure, religion, ideologies, etc...these things will always be flawed due to that very simple variable being 'humans'. Human beings bring emotions into play and with emotions often times come irrational ways of thinking and doing things. What do I mean by this? One irrational action to me is how can we pretend to take a stand against wrongs taking place states away when we won't even leave from one room in our homes to the next to correct the wrongs that reside there? And if we do truly feel moved and compelled to attack these social injustices, I'm sure we should feel an even greater desire to right as many of the wrongs that we face in our day-to-day life.   Just food for thought as I awaken to this Sunday's sun.

LSohl
12/21/14

The Eight-sided Race

With endless negative media coverage and tremendous assistance from many in the Black community, we have conditioned all races including our own to view us as a faceless people. Through psychological projection, many in the Western world displace their insecurities, desires, and shortcomings onto the Black race. Blacks men are said to be lustful of the White woman. Blacks are lazy. Blacks are feebleminded, low-hanging fruit in society, etc. These degrading and false stigmas and images have been placed upon the Black race by the White society for generations. This was a brilliant campaign of dehumanizing/devaluing us as a people. To understand the cleverness in this approach, again we must understand the profound effect of conditioning a mind, and also how the average psyche operates. We must entertain the behavioral studies of placing any stigma (whether negative or positive) on an individual or people, and through time and a constant placement of said stigma, the individual or people will embrace the behaviors.

To question the veracity of these Western ideologies and misconceptions then expose the many falsehoods of such allegations would be a minute point for one simple reason..."Mechanics of a Nigga"! But, I will discuss in some detail a few of the tactics and how we have succumbed to White society's depiction of us.

Let's begin with some of the aforementioned stigmas. Laziness. Off the backs of countless Blacks during American slavery, this country prospered. Whites have an uneasiness accepting this fact. They would like to shed light on a numerical point that of the millions of Africans transported to the Western world during the Transatlantic Slave trade, not even a half million landed in what is labeled America. What White America does not want to digest is the fact of that over four million Black slaves were "freed" (freed being stressed in satire) with the Emancipation Proclamation. This proves that after generation of free Black backbreaking labor, Blacks helped build a nation that we have no legal stock or claim to. Now, this feebleminded attribute is easily canceled out by the countless revolutionary inventions and contributions made by the Black race. And in reflecting back on psychological projection and the reaction formation, we can look into the denial, guilt, and insecurities of White America and explore their belief of all Black men lusting over the White female.

The White race realizes that genetically they can be extinct if race mixing continues. They know that the melanin possessed by the Black man is the most dominant of all people of color, and that this skin-color producing component will eventually wipe out their entire "superior" race as they know it. These anxieties produce fear, resentment and hate towards the Black race. To prevent such extremes, they have to hate what they cannot generate...this dominate melanin trait. They begin to despise this desire they all have to obtain some form of skin color, and the lust their White females have for the Black man so they can procreate and with the Black man to produce children of color...something the White man can never do. They resent the fact that they cannot obtain these things naturally. Many have artificially sought out ways to obtain skin color through sun tanning and usage of chemical toxins. These forms of resentment are better understood when exploring facets of the reaction formation and psychological displacement.

But through White society's perpetual campaign of propagating such ideologies, many Blacks have allowed these falsehoods to plague their minds and restructure their social behaviors. They take on these depictions and live them out. Numerous Black men sought after the" forbidden fruit"...White women. Black reality shows depict us as buffoons, idiots, hot-temperament clowns with little aspirations. Many take to social media and display the same by posting video clips of our Black sisters dancing distastefully, and senseless physical altercations amongst our own. Countless crimes and homicides are committed within our own race. Many within the Black race contribute to this modern day genocide with homosexuality acts, homicide, drug usage, and criminal activities that places them in the penal system which eventually destroys the Black family structure. I will note that the poverty-stricken and ghetto situations many Blacks reside in do contribute to crime. Joblessness produces such. This is not a race thing but more so a social epidemic that takes place whenever there is a situation of being without...self-preservation. And White America has placed us in these ghettos and poverty-stricken communities.

Now, with the White media's campaign to expose us as a negative and simple-minded race of people combined with the Black on Black crime, we have become somewhat faceless. The killing of Blacks by racist White police officers doesn't resonate as barbaric and inhuman to White society when reported on the news. It has become more of a "norm" than anything else. White America has all but erased whatever cognitive dissonance they may have had in killing Blacks in this country. Uneducated Blacks have even rid themselves of their cognitive dissonance when criminalizing and killing each other.

I liken the Black race current situation to the stop sign. We all are taught different shapes at an early age in elementary school. One particular shape we all learned is the octagon (eight-side). But after years and years of seeing the octagon shape being painted red and white and used as one of the many signs to regulate the flow of traffic, we have conditioned our minds to replace the octagon shape with the term stop sign whenever we see it. This is what mind conditioning does. And through all the negative media, stigmas, and misconceptions that have been placed on Blacks in American society, we are no longer viewed as humans but as faceless shells of little to no worth. We have become the octagon turned stop sign in this society. This is a subject taboo to the masses because many are uncomfortable with this reality. But what can be comfortable and easy about a racist system? Racism is an inhuman, cruel, unjust, barbaric and daily practice by White America that must be addressed.

Western society (White America) frowns at its own moral hygiene. It reeks of a fowl, rotten, and decaying stench that pollutes this nation and many nations. This society's morality smells from its racist toil.

Can I live? (blog)

When Blacks want to organize and obtain businesses, and communities of our own, Whites view this as Blacks being racist, subversive to a "fair" democratic government, and militant. Blacks cannot be racist...they can employ many prejudices, but lack the social status power to affect another race's livelihood. Blacks wanting to not depend on the very racist society that categorizes them as 2nd class, and denies them, even today, human God-given rights and fair treatment under the political, judicial, social, and moral system defined by Western standards of law and conduct is not an act of being unpatriotic, but instead rebelling for a change.

For Blacks to work towards being independent from such unfair and unjust treatment by the White racist society that lives in denial then ask the question "why" or pose such an outrageous and illogical reply claiming reverse racism on the part of Blacks is an asinine comparison. This would be equivalent to the murderous wolf seeking justice against the helpless sheep it has/does preys upon its entire life. No more can the sheep, who has been hunted and used as a delicacy to line the stomach of this greedy, cunning, and vicious beast, be labeled the aggressor and violator against the wolf can the Black man in American be labeled a racist.

Racism exits in both the infrastructure and superstructure, conscious and unconscious of most Western White society today. Modern racism is practiced with discretion and tact, and employed by disproportionate percentages of minority incarcerations within the penal system, police brutality against unarmed Blacks and people of color, the unemployment rates in Black communities, the living conditions in the Black communities, the unequal opportunities in the work force to obtain high positions Blacks qualify for, and the poor education of Blacks. It's not being a racist when Blacks want to break free of such a stronghold over them. That's called being sensible and smart!

The Non-tangible
In theory

Hate, love, fear, comfort, joy, sadness; all defined as emotions, unexplained, non-tangible energies with ties and origins to both the conscious and subconscious thoughts...residing in the left and right hemisphere of the brain. These various emotions attribute to individual actions, interactions, logic, speech, beliefs, etc. These unseen, existences are as much a reality as the air we breathe, and they affect every aspect of our lives.

Take for example the collective's need for appropriate personal space, with the exception of family, friends, and lovers, in order for each and every individual to feel comfortable in both a public and private setting. We must first pose the question what is this personal space? How is it measured, and by what apparatus can we measure this non-tangible need? And what happens when this need is not meet and someone invades our personal space? This cognition and perception shared by the collective has been established and agreed upon internally in the amygdala ganglion of the brain, and requires that this need is met physically in order for the collective to "feel" secure and comfort. If these needs are not met, the collective displays resistance, discomfort, annoyance, irritability, uneasiness, tension, and an array of negative energies produce in the infrastructure then exhibited externally through the superstructure. 'Bright' emotions collapse and give way to feelings of anger. Are these needs permanent, or can the collective be conditioned to redefine individual comfort when referring to required personal space? Or can these "needed barriers" be eliminated altogether?

We must first acknowledge that there is a conscious switch and barrier formed to alert and secure individual personal space. Once we acknowledge this, we must define it in order to establish if such a need is a need after all. In defining, we learn the laws of operation, its origin, and make-up, and in doing so we can manipulate these laws or recondition in an effort to minimize, control, or eliminate the pseudo-need permanently.

Personal spaces vary depending on the relationship with others, culture, regions, and uncontrolled situations. In uncontrolled situations such as crowned public transportation, personal spaces are definitely encroached upon. But studies have shown that during these times, people feel their violators/intruders are irrelevant or pose no threat. So, this uneasy feeling can be controlled!

Now, how does all of this place us on the 'road to Rome'...my metonymy to racism? I suggest the re-patterning and reprogramming of society through teaching and cultural cleansing which would produced a society conditioned in the likeness of a colonized euphoria. Of course this is but a child-like dream due to the countless human, civil, biological, and mental factors involved which would be met with unpredictable resistance. However, in some cases I theorize that being able to manipulate the laws of personal space which intertwine with several emotions, including feelings of security, joy, or their opposites which are many of the same feelings closely related to racist mentalities, then we can also define racism and the

laws which govern these ideals and beliefs of pseudo-superiority,
entitlement, infringement, abandonment, resistance, envy, hate, etc., that resides in
the distorted minds of individuals. In doing this we will be able to redefine
said energies in willing participants...key word 'willing'.

Great theory to me- asinine to others.

EXPIRED
Reality or Dream? (blog)

Today's society has catapulted itself to a makeshift social stratosphere where it now looks down from a pretend exosphere in its parallel reality to see Divine. It has deviated from its very foundation, hoisted itself past the shoulders of sound and traditional morals, integrity, and any and all spiritual and factual accounts while we, the old, have stood by and allowed the "new" to redefine practically every facet of life; love, hate, good, bad, blessings and sins in accordance to orthodox holy doctrines. A sullen satire to older generations upbringing has manifested as the essence of true living- a tasteless mockery of core social principles. What has been ushered into our living rooms as laws, standards, "the new ways", are nothing more than the "new" popular opinions that are in the majority...as of now. Now, so many of the old step aside, fade away, or blend in; conforming to gentile etiquettes and culture...feebleness. Living a life in the fast lane, operating and blind-maneuvering an even faster car. RECKLESS!!!

Again, I find myself at a common place in a common space in my life; solitude...to still the raging waves of emotions within in an effort to find the questions and answers needed to remedy such morally unjust practices. So I begin viewing it all from a business aspect; risk versus the reward, and weigh the options and outcomes, pros and cons. Things look extremely grim, darker than I've ever seen as I meticulously search for all factors to generate a positive outcome. I'm cognizant of this race of the races. I'm aware of facts versus opinions, the spectrum of personalities, moral and amoral handles, etc. I conclude it is a job called for a blurred demigod with a bloodline mainly of a supreme deity...me.

So I sit impatiently in the Lorraine hotel...dozing! Next morning I stand on the hotel's balcony yearning while I'm knowing my position; my people's new vanguard for community programs to heal, feed, uplift, educate, and recondition our minds and spirituality in order to breathe clean air into clear thinking. I have to bring attention to these killing fields constructed by so many of my people as well as the police and various government agencies. I have to expose every race of people to these injustices and recondition the minds and hearts to embrace John Donne's quote/question "for whom the bell tows?" I have to prove to the world that the minute differences in their religious practices pull society as a whole from connecting to a Divine spirituality. Enriched proverbs must be digested and exercised. Social theories must become strict factual living. Then it hits me as a sharp pain simultaneously hits me in the neck and chest. OUR TIME IS UP!!!

Natural Order

So, in retrospect, what is "it" all about? I would say peace...peace of mind. In concluding this, we must first address the "what" meaning what we are as oppose to who we are. We are members of the human race. Humans, by nature, are curious beings and the defining nature of all that exist is conflict. These are things we must fully acknowledge and comprehend before we can find this peace of mind. While focusing on peace as it pertains to our curious nature, we as humans must find answers to the unknowns of our very limited minds when compared to Divine energy that is "All...always has and always will be".

We made agreements from the very beginning of time to explain occurrences in the natural order of life. These agreements will continue to have a profound impact on present and distant-future living in this society. We have agreed upon labels, terms, and definitions to coin and box life as we know it in an effort to give it meaning perhaps we can understand. We've constructed multi-directional marks and lines that have been agreed upon to be labeled letters, which in turn are placed in a particular order then called words. These words have been given meaning and the meaning of each word had to be agreed upon by society as a collective in order to establish a written form of communication which brings understanding to unknowns. We have agreed as a collective to the different pitches and sounds used by humans to create a form of auditory communication, sign language and brail for the deaf and blind. All of these, along with countless other agreements condition each individual and this society as a whole.

Agreements made have to represent some form and level of importance to us both objective and/or subjectively. Prices placed upon any marketed item represents this society's supply and demand philosophy, which simply put exposes the importance we place on any particular item. This "importance" can be said for each and every agreement we make or have made in our lives- past, present, and future. The middle finger, for instance, has to be agreed upon subjectively to be offensive when gestured by an upset individual towards another. Some have allowed this simple motion to have significant importance in their lives to the point it affects their emotions and often time provokes a negative response whether verbally or physically from the offended...sometimes both. Racist propaganda, i.e., flags, symbols, labels, and slurs have to be agreed upon by the offender and the offended if its intent is to be successful. Imagine if the offended would recondition their thought process and shift the level of importance to zero when faced with such asinine behaviors by the offenders. Then we would have to redefine both roles. No longer would emotions be involved when referencing the offended. Needless to say, we would have neither the offender or offended. The offender's role can only stay the same if he/she becomes physically aggressive which then brings to surface the natural defense mechanism of the offended and all living species...self preservation. This natural tendency is exhibited with and without feelings being present.

Now, human feelings, as we have labeled these daily non-tangible experiences, are said to be subjective. But a closer look reveals in the conscious mind, society collective has moved some feelings into the objective category. Take love for instance. As big of a meaning love has, we have consciously manufactured a general mold when describing to ourselves and others what should be expected…as if this EMOTION, along with any emotion, can truly be so generic and defined as such. And in doing so, if these prerequisites aren't meet then "love" simply is not there for the conditioned heart. Note: There are the select few which has redefined what love means to them and the importance they have placed on such a feeling.

We use terms like life in order explain death, good to explain bad, light to explain dark and so forth. But what exactly is life? What is death? When looking at the grand scale of things in terms of Diving powers, can these things be readily defined? Here is something to consider and digest. Would there be a thing called life if all things in nature moved infinitely even if at different speeds? Movement is a basic principle in physics. If this was the case, would there be motion, and what is motion but the change in the position of any object in regards to time (Time having no value in infinity). So death, as we would label the motionless would be a body at rest I presume. Death, in this case, would not exit, nor would life. What then, would our limited minds agree upon to call such a state of being? I only mention this to further point out agreements we have made to try and explain the many "unknowns" we run into while feeding our natural state of curiosity. The curious nature of all humans leads us to seek answers to unknown. These answers provide a sense of peace within us all.

Good, evil, right, wrong…all things subjectively defined and boxed into a term called morals to try and mask the reality of what the very nature of the human species is…beings of conflict. The world exists because of conflict. Every organism, species, race, creed, color; whatever the living phylum may be, exits because of external and/or internal conflict. I have led you to this point in an effort to assist you in reconditioning your brain's computer while in life's journey. This point is of the greatest importance because in our search for individual peace and as a collective society, we must understand what we are as oppose to who we are. We are humans before we are placed into any race or ethnic group. Conflict residing in the natural order of life leads us to our greatest peace. Understanding, and embracing this understanding of how conflict and peace are one in the same in the natural order of existence brings about more clarity to the "unknowns". My cousin says that understanding the natural order of life as oppose to attempting to change something that cannot be changed (the natural order of life) is peace within itself. He stresses that if one changes their mind then they change their reality.

Dress code (blog)

I woke feeling a high...colorful and energized so I scramble towards my closet to arrange my attire that will reflect the same. I want to present and project these good vibes to this world I'm about to encounter. On days not so bright to me, my clothes are arranged in similar fashion; to reflect my feelings. Funny how my mind works though, because at times when I'm feeling down, I'd go shopping to lift my spirit, so-to-speak. Ambivalent? Nah. Well yes! Wait! Ah, I don't know. Maybe we can ascribe these ups and downs (emotions) as conflict that dwells naturally within us all. And through empirical living and existing we can conclude that the very nature of human beings is based around conflict.

Our emotions; fear, hate, love, joy, etc., are of a contradictory nature. Yet we possess them all and they often times more than seldom, clash and intertwine with one another. Emotions are as big a part of the make-up of human beings as the epidermis, tissues, fluids, organs, and bones that clothes our existence.

Now, in this primal civilization we coexist in, the majority collective has made agreements as to define what is "normal society". And in cutting out this pattern/mold, we have what's known in layman terms as the subjective conscious. Envy, greed, lust, sloth, gluttony, pride, empathy, and jealousy...all attributes created by a majority to define what's considered a moral compass. We're not going to get so caught up in personal jargon and/or the lexicon due to it might cause a distraction from the point being made. CONFLICT! Put that word to the side (but not too far) for a second and let's move back to our clothing.

You see, in normal society our clothes often plays a major role in where we are and where we are trying to go if not representing who we are in this world...business attire often times representing a business man or woman, sport apparel tethering a physically active individual (noted: not all times in either case), hip-hop clothing mirroring that hip-hop attitude in the person wearing such. So, we have agreed to define ourselves to a degree by the clothes we wear. But, in addressing this from somewhat of a psychological aspect the clothing as in its fundamental purpose only covers the individual. It defines the "who" which is what the collective society has agreed upon in reference to this subjective conscious.

We are influenced from birth in the defining of our "who". From the impressions made by our parents, teachers, ministers, coaches, idiot boxes, and every other form of media, we consciously and subconscious cut and paste to define who we are in an effort to be accepted by "normal society". BUT the important factor we so often over look while spending our entire life searching to define who we are, we skip the very first step of nature...what we are. We are humans, and we are at a constant conflict with each other and ourselves whether speaking physical, emotional, spiritual, or mental. That's what we do. (Back to the conflict)

We have attempted to create religions and morals as the "who" to clothed the what. This takes me back to the story told of the Good Samaritan lady coming across a dying snake, and takes it into her home then nurses the snake back to health. One day, the lady comes home to find the healthy snake closest her feet. To her surprise, he snake strikes her with no hesitation. She is said to have looked down at the snake and ask why, "Why would you bite me after all I have done for you?" The snake replied, "Bitch, I'm still a snake!" It, as we and every other living organism on this planet, cannot go against the very nature that defines us.

Human are the only confused species on this planet. Every other species acknowledges and follow its natural order of existing and coexisting. The primal human beings believe they can change or rearrange the "what" with the "who". I beg to differ. By me clothing a dog in a tailored three-piece suit will not stop it from barking, chasing cats, and pissing on fire hydrants nor will it turn the canine into a business(Man). Know the difference, and flirt with the subjective conscious...even embrace it if you will.

In life, we all pretty much experience most of the same situations and similar circumstances that triggers our natural emotions. Now, how each individual deals with his/her emotions define that person's character in referencing this moral compass "normal society" has agreed upon as a majority collective. Wear your clothes proudly, the mental subjective conscious and these man made garments. Just know that there is a major difference in defining the two. Now of course I have to pose these questions before I go. What is in your mental closet? And what clothes do you wear?

Thoughts of LSohl & Doc
©LSohl 2015
All Rights Reserved
10/15/15

Log on and like www.facebook.com/LostSohl to stay up on my lastest post

and follow me on **Twitter @Lsohl1** and **Instagram @tim_hollins**